ISBN 978-0-266-08045-9
PIBN 10948357

For support please visit www.forgottenbooks.com

1 MONTH OF
FREE
READING

at
www.ForgottenBooks.com

By purchasing this book you are eligible for one month membership to ForgottenBooks.com, giving you unlimited access to our entire collection of over 1,000,000 titles via our web site and mobile apps.

To claim your free month visit:

www.forgottenbooks.com/free948357

English
Français
Deutsche
Italiano
Español
Português

www.forgottenbooks.com

Mythology Photography **Fiction**
Fishing Christianity **Art** Cooking
Essays Buddhism Freemasonry
Medicine **Biology** Music **Ancient**
Egypt Evolution Carpentry Physics
Dance Geology **Mathematics** Fitness
Shakespeare **Folklore** Yoga Marketing
Confidence Immortality Biographies
Poetry **Psychology** Witchcraft
Electronics Chemistry History **Law**
Accounting **Philosophy** Anthropology
Alchemy Drama Quantum Mechanics
Atheism Sexual Health **Ancient History**
Entrepreneurship Languages Sport
Paleontology Needlework Islam
Metaphysics Investment Archaeology
Parenting Statistics Criminology
Motivational

BOSTON COLLEGE

THE

College of Arts and Sciences

The College of Arts and Sciences offers courses leading o the degrees of Bachelor of Arts and Bachelor of Science. In he Bachelor of Arts course the following fields of concentration ire open to election: Biology, Classics, Economics, Education, .nglish, German, Business Studies, Government, History, Legal itudies, Mathematics, Philosophy, Physics, Romance Languages, Social Studies.

In the Bachelor of Science course fields of concentration nay be chosen from Biology, Chemistry, Physics, Education, Iistory, Economics, Government, and Sociology.

For Further Information Kindly Address

JOHN P. FOLEY, S.J., Dean of Freshmen
Boston College
Chestnut Hill, Massachusetts

Telephone BIGelow 1480

BOSTON COLLEGE BULLETIN

APRIL, 1941

Volume XIII

Number 3

Summer School of Arts and Sciences and of Education

June 30th to August 8th, 1941

UNIVERSITY HEIGHTS
CHESTNUT HILL, MASSACHUSETTS

Boston College Bulletin

Bulletins issued in each volume:

No. 1, February (Entrance-College of Arts and Sciences) February (Entrance-School of Business Administration); No. (Summer School); No. 4, April (Law School); No. 5, April of Social Work); No. 6, July (Intown Division); No. 7, (Graduate School); No. 8, October (General Catalogue); October (School of Business Administration).

Entered as second-class matter February 28, 1929, at the post office at Boston, Massachusetts, under the act of August 24, 1912.

Published by
BOSTON COLLEGE
140 COMMONWEALTH AVENUE
CHESTNUT HILL
NEWTON, MASSACHUSETTS
BIGelow 1480

BOSTON COLLEGE BULLETIN

~⚭⚭~

Summer School of Arts and Sciences and of Education

JUNE 30 to AUGUST 8, 1941

Published by Boston College

CHESTNUT HILL, MASS.

1941

TABLE OF CONTENTS

Calendar

Faculty

General Information

For the Degree of Bachelor

For the Degree of Master

Registration and Fees

Outline of Courses

Accounting

Biology

Chemistry

Dramatic Arts

Economics

Education

English

French

Gaelic

German

Greek

History and Government

Italian

Latin

Mathematics

Philosophy

Physics

Religion

Sociology

Spanish

Schedule of Courses

CALENDAR

SUMMER SESSION, 1941

23-28, Registration at Boston College, Chestnut Hill;
  June 23-27: 9-12 A. M., 2-5 P. M.
  June 28: 9-12 A. M.

A Late Registration Fee of two dollars will be required of all ents without exception who register after the time assigned.

30 Formal opening of the summer session,
  Library auditorium, 8:45 A. M.
  All classes begin at the hours announced.

4 Holiday—classes do not meet.

7-8 Examination period.
  Classes are held daily, Monday through Friday.

SUMMER SCHOOL

Officers of Administration

President—REVEREND WILLIAM J. MURPHY, S.J.

Director-Graduate Division—REVEREND GEORGE A. O'DONNELL, S.J.

Registrar, Graduate Division—FRANCIS J. CAMPBELL, A.M.

Director, Undergraduate Division—REVEREND VINCENT DE P. O'BRIEN, S.J.

Registrar, Undergraduate Division—FREDERICK A. NORTON, A.B.

FACULTY

EDUARDO AZUOLA, Litt.D., Ph.D., *Spanish*
REV. HENRY A. BEAN, S.J., *English*
REV. CAROL L. BERNHARDT, S.J., *English*
REV. FREDERICK W. BOEHM, S.J., *Philosophy*
REV. JOHN L.-BONN, S.J., *Dramatic Arts*
PAUL A. BOULANGER, Ph.D., *German*
REV. JAMES L. BRENNAN, S.J., *English*
FREDERICK T. BRYAN, M.B.A, *Accounting*
ROBERT J. BUCK, M.F.S., *Economics*
REV. CHARLES E. BUCKLEY, S.J., *Greek*
REV. JAMES L. BURKE, S.J., *History*
ANNA P. BUTLER, Ph.D., *Education*
REV. WILLIAM M. CAREY, S.J., *Philosophy*
REV. ANTHONY G. CARROLL, S.J., *Chemistry*
NAZZARENO CEDRONE, M.S., *Mathematics*
REV. JOHN J. COLLINS, S.J., *Religion*
REV. PATRICK H. COLLINS, S.J., *English*
REV. TERENCE L. CONNOLLY, S.J., *English*
REV. FRANCIS J. COTTER, S.J., *Philosophy*
REV. EDWARD T. DOUGLAS, S.J., *Religion*
HARRY M. DOYLE, Ph.D., *History*
REV. JOHN F. DOHERTY, S.J., *Education*
JOHN J. DRUMMEY, M.B.A., *Accounting*
REV. EVAN C. DUBOIS, S.J., *Biology*
REV. ALEXANDER G. DUNCAN, S.J., *Philosophy*
ELIOT K. DUVEY, B.S., *Dramatic Arts*
HAROLD FAGAN, M.S., *Chemistry*
REV. THOMAS B. FEENEY, S.J., *English*
REV. EDWARD H. FINNEGAN, S.J., *History*
REV. LEON E. FITZGERALD, S.J., *French*
REV. W. E. FITZGERALD, S.J., *Latin*

George F. Fitzgibbon, Ph.D., *Sociology*
Rev. Francis Flaherty, S.J., *Philosophy*
Rev. Joseph P. Fox, S.J., *Education*
Rev. Walter F. Friary, S.J., *Philosophy*
F. Malcolm Gager, E.E., *Physics*
Rev. James F. Geary, S.J., *History*
Miriam G. Gow, B.Ed., *Choral Speaking*
G. F. Gage Grob, A.M., *English*
Frederick J. Guerin, Ph.D., *Chemistry*
Rev. Ferdinand W. Haberstroh, S.J., *Philosophy*
Rev. Michael J. Harding, S.J., *Philosophy*
Rev. Martin P. Harney, S.J., *History*
Mary A. Haverty, M.Ed., *Education*
John J. Hayes, A.M., *French*
Rev. Laurence F. Herne, S.J., *Latin*
Rev. Patrick J. Higgins, S.J., *History*
Rev. William L. Johnson, S.J., *English*
Wylma R. Kellar, Ph.D., *Education*
Rev. Stephen A. Koen, S.J., *Education*
Erich N. Labouvie, *German*
Rev. John A. McCarthy, S.J., *Philosophy*
Rev. Leo P. McCauley, S.J., *Latin*
Rev. Albert F. McGuinn, S.J., *Chemistry*
Rev. James D. McLaughlin, S.J., *Religion*
Thomas D. Mahoney, A.M., *History*
Rev. Paul deMangeleere, S.J., *French*
Rene J. Marcou, B.S., *Mathematics*
Francis L. Maynard, A.M., *Biology*
Rev. James J. Mohan, S.J., *Philosophy*
Rev. Stephen A. Mulcahy, S.J., *Latin*
Rev. John E. Murphy, S.J., *Gaelic*
Rev. John J. Murphy, S.J., *Philosophy*
Rev. John A. O'Brien, S.J., *Philosophy*
Rev. Daniel F. X. O'Connor, S.J., *Philosophy*
Rev. John C. O'Connell, S.J., *Sociology*
David C. O'Donnell, Ph.D., *Chemistry*
Rev. Thomas J. Quinn, S.J., *Latin*
Rev. Oswald A. Reinhalter, S.J., *Latin*
Hans Reinheimmer, Ph.D., *Physics*
Thomas I. Ryan, M.S., *Biology*
Rev. Richard G. Shea, S.J., *Latin*
Rev. Stephen A. Shea, S.J., *Philosophy*
Gino deSolenni, Ph.D., *Italian*
Leon M. Vincent, M.S., *Biology*
Frederick E. White, Ph.D., *Physics*

GENERAL INFORMATION

For Candidates for the Degree of Bachelor
at BOSTON COLLEGE INTOWN

On the opposite page may be found a composite chart of requirements for students aspiring to the Bachelor's degree at Boston College Intown. The purpose of the curriculum therein presented is to provide for the student an *integrated* and *progressive* course of studies in conformity with the Jesuit *"Ratio Studiorum."* The requirements for degrees have been adjusted to harmonize as closely as possible with those prevailing in the central College of Liberal Arts and Sciences at Chestnut Hill. The following points are called to the attention of students for a correct understanding of the chart.

1) The curriculum representing a total of one hundred and twenty (120) semester hours credit, has been divided into four (4) stadia or brackets each of which represents a total of thirty (30) semester hours credit.

2) Candidates for degrees will be required to complete the courses assigned to the first bracket (I) before passing on to the courses assigned to the second bracket (II), and so on with respect to the other brackets (III and IV).

3) In the case of students who transfer with advanced standing from other accredited colleges, it will be required that they complete whatever courses they lack in the first bracket (I) before taking courses in the second bracket (II), and so on with respect to the other brackets (III and IV).

4) During the regular scholastic year students will be allowed to carry a program of studies not exceeding eighteen (18) semester hours credit. During a single semester no student will be allowed to carry a program exceeding ten (10) semester hours credit.

5) During the Summer Session candidates for degrees will be allowed to carry a program of studies not exceeding six (6) semester hours credit.

6) A maximum of eight (8) years will be allowed for the completion of the required one hundred and twenty (120) semester hours. A minimum of six (6) years will be required for the same purpose.

7) Four degrees are offered under this curriculum, namely, Bachelor of Arts, Bachelor of Science in Education, Bachelor of Science in History, and Bachelor of Science in Social Science.

achelor of Arts		Subjects	Bachelor of Science		
			A	B	C
(I)	3	Philosophy: Dialectics	3	3	3
	3	Philosophy: Epistemology	3	3	3
	2	Ontology	2	2	2
	2	Latin: Composition	..	..	..
	2	Cicero: Pro Archia & Pro Marcello	..	..	..
	2	Horace: Odes	..	..	..
	..	Educational Orientation	2	..	..
	..	Educational Psychology	2	..	..
	..	English: Composition	4	4	4
	4	English: Art of Poetry	4	4	4
	4	History: Early Christian	4	4	4
	..	History: English	..	4	4
	6	Greek or Mathematics	4	4	4
30 credits	2	Religion: Divinity of Christ	2	2	2

(A) in Education
(B) in History
(C) in Social Science

	2	Philosophy: Cosmology	2	2	2
	2	Philosophy: Fundamental Psychol.	2	2	2
	2	Philosophy: Advanced Psychology	2	2	2
	2	Cicero: Pro Lege Manilia	..	..	..
	2	Horace & Juvenal: Satires	..	..	..
	2	Tacitus: Agricola & Annales	..	..	..
(II)	..	Education: History of	4	..	..
	4	English: Art of Rhetoric	4	4	4
	4	English: History of Literature	4	4	4
	..	English: Contemporary American	2	2	2
	4	History: Middle Ages	4	4	4
	..	History: American	..	4	4
	4	Modern Language	4	4	4
30 credits	2	Religion: Church of Christ	2	2	2

	4	Philosophy: General Ethics	4	4	4
	4	Philosophy: Special Ethics	4	4	4
	..	Education: Principles of	2	..	..
	..	Education: General Methods	2	..	..
	..	English: Shakespeare	..	4	..
	2	History: Renaissance	2	2	2
(III)	2	History: Reformation	2	2	2
	4	Modern Language	4	4	4
	6	Science: Lectures & Lab.	6	6	6
	..	Sociology: Fundamental	..	..	4
	6	Electives	2	2	2
30 credits	2	Religion: The Redemption	2	2	2

	2	Philosophy: Natural Theology	2	2	2
	4	Philosophy: History of	4	4	4
	4	Modern Language	4	4	4
(IV)	..	Education	8	..	..
	..	History	..	8	..
	..	Sociology	..	..	8
	18	Electives	10	10	10
30 credits	2	Religion: The Sacraments	2	2	2

Note: This chart is subject to minor changes.

For Candidates for the Degree of Master

The Graduate School accepts properly qualified candidates for the degree of Master of Arts, Master of Science, and Master of Education.

After admission to the Graduate School, the student must spend at least one full year in residence, pursuing the courses approved by the Dean and the student's adviser. Students who are engaged in outside work which reduces the time and thought they are able to give to study will be required to devote more than the minimum time to their study for the degree.

For the Master's degree, a student must secure a minimum of thirty semester hours of graduate credit in approved courses. To receive graduate credit, a grade of A or B (80-100) must be attained.

The candidate for a graduate degree must at the time of his matriculation, make choice of the department in which he wishes to do his principal or major work. In his choice of a department, the candidate is restricted to the fields of study in which he has had the necessary preparation in his college courses. In addition, the student must satisfy the special prerequisite requirements of his major department.

The entire program of studies which a student offers in fulfillment of the requirements for a degree must be satisfactorily completed within a period of six years from the date when he first registered. Should a candidate for any reason whatsoever fail to receive his degree within the time prescribed, all claim or right to continue working for the degree, or to have any or all of the work already accomplished credited in fulfillment of the requirements for the same degree, is ipso facto forfeited and annulled.

A very important part of the work for a degree is the thesis on some subject in the field of the candidate's major work. Two copies of an outline of the thesis, with the written approval of the professor under whose direction it is to be done, must be furnished to the Dean before the first of January of the scholastic year in which the degree is to be conferred. These outlines must be submitted on the forms supplied by the Graduate School office.

No thesis will be accepted for a Master's degree which is confined to the mere compilation of facts derived from the writings of others, nor will merely literary combinations of such information be acceptable. The thesis must show originality in the treatment of the subject chosen. This original treatment must give evidence that the writer of the thesis is capable of opening a new field of investigation, or of offering such critical opinion that a real advance is made in the study of the subject treated.

In the preparation of the thesis, the candidate must observe the regulations in regard to forms of citation, footnotes, and the like, as set forth in the mimeographed instructions prepared by the Board of Graduate Studies.

Each candidate must furnish two bound typewritten or printed copies of his thesis to the College Library. These copies become the property of the College. The typewritten copies must be on paper of a uniform size 8 inches by $10\frac{1}{2}$ inches.

Written examinations in the different courses followed are required of the candidate on the completion of each course. A final comprehensive oral examination upon all work presented for the degree is also required.

Special Requirements for the Degree of Master

For information regarding the special requirements for the various degrees of Master offered by the Graduate School of Boston College consult the Bulletin of the Graduate School or address the Dean of the Graduate School, Boston College, Chestnut Hill, Mass.

Registration

The days assigned for formal registration are June 23-28. During June, the office of the School in the Tower Building, Boston College, Chestnut Hill, Mass., will be open every day except Saturdays from 2.00 to 5.00 in the afternoon.

Courses

A candidate for the degree of Bachelor will not be permitted to take more than three courses (six semester hours).

A candidate for the degree of Master will not be permitted to take more than two courses (four semester hours).

Fees

Matriculation Fee: New students	$ 5.00
Old students	1.00
Fee for each course per semester hour	10.00
Laboratory Fee by arrangement	
Library Fee: Undergraduate students	2.00
Graduate students per semester hour	1.00
Late registration fee	2.00

Attendance

Absence from more than ten per cent of the lecture or seminar periods renders the candidate ineligible for credits for the course in question.

Withdrawal from Classes

Any student withdrawing from a course must notify the Dean immediately.

N. B. *The Faculty reserves the right to withdraw any of the courses in which there is not a registration of fifteen students.*

Information

For information concerning graduate courses address the Registrar, Graduate Division; for undergraduate courses address the Registrar, Undergraduate Division, Boston College, Chestnut Hill, Mass.

Courses of Instruction

Courses numbered 1 to 99 are strictly undergraduate courses. Credit earned in these courses is applicable only to the Bachelor's degree.

Courses numbered 100-199 are open to advanced undergraduate students and to graduate students.

Courses numbered 200-299 are strictly graduate courses and open only to graduate students.

ACCOUNTING

ACCOUNTING 1. ELEMENTARY ACCOUNTING, I.

This course presents the basic principles necessary for an intelligent understanding of the books and records used in business. The following subjects are discussed: principles of debits and credits, opening and closing books, classification and analysis of accounts, controlling accounts, the voucher system, trial balance, working papers, preparation and analysis of financial statements.

Daily, 9:55-10:45.   Two semester hours.
                                                            Mr. BRYAN.

ACCOUNTING 2. ELEMENTARY ACCOUNTING, II.

This course is a continuation of Accounting 1. It covers the account development of different forms of business organizations which include the individual proprietorships, partnerships and corporations. The trading and manufacturing operations of these types of business organizations are presented. Consideration is given to problems of asset and liability analysis.

Daily, 11:45-12:35.   Two semester hours.
                                                            Mr. BRYAN.

ACCOUNTING 21. INTERMEDIATE ACCOUNTING, I.

This course provides a logical continuation of the elementary courses. Stress is laid on the various problems involved in the preparation of financial statements both as to the form of statement and the basis of valuation of the various items included therein. Emphasis will be placed on consideration of executive policy with regard to accounting practice.

Daily, 9:00-9:50.   Two semester hours.
                                                            Prof. DRUMMEY.

ACCOUNTING 22. INTERMEDIATE ACCOUNTING, II.

Among the subjects to be treated are: funds and reserves, installment sales, branch office and subsidiary accounting mergers, receiverships and estate and trust accounting.

Daily, 10:50-11:40.   Two semester hours.
                                                            Prof. DRUMMEY.

BIOLOGY

BIOLOGY 2. GENERAL BIOLOGY.

The aim of this course is to give a biological background to philosophical, sociological and educational studies. It includes such important topics as properties of living organisms, from the lowest to the most complex in both plants and animals.

Daily, one lecture and two hours laboratory.   Four semester hours.
                                            Prof. VINCENT and his Assistants.

BIOLOGY 3. GENETICS.

A lecture course on heredity. The object of the course is to study and analyze the facts upon which fundamental principles of inheritance are based. These facts will be taken from the sphere of plant and animal breeding. Application to human characters will be made wherever facts warrant. Demonstrations, charts and lantern slides will supplement the data of the lectures. Supplementary work for the student will be required in practice problems, discussion of assigned topics and review questions.

Daily, 10:50-11:40.   Two semester hours.
                                                             Prof. DuBois, S.J.

BIOLOGY 4. HYGIENE.

This course will include a discussion of the organization and workings of various systems of the body, and of the hygenic measures necessary to keep them in the best working order. The role of the internal and external agents adversely affecting the health of the body will be discussed, especially from the point of view of prevention.

Daily, 11:45-12:35.   Two semester hours.
                                                             Mr. RYAN.

BIOLOGY 5. PHYSIOLOGY.

This course will consist of lectures and demonstrations. The subject matter will include Man and his relations to his environment both internal and external. The following topics will be considered: Digestion, Circulation, Respiration, Secretion, Sensation, Vitamins, Hormones, Enzymes, the effect of Radiant Energy, Locomotion, Age and Death. Demonstrations will be given by the instructor and members of the class to illustrate certain of the phenomena discussed in class.

Daily, 12:40-1:30.   Two semester hours.
                                                             Mr. MAYNARD.

CHEMISTRY

CHEMISTRY 1. GENERAL INORGANIC CHEMISTRY.

This is an introductory course which aims to cover the general field of Inorganic Chemistry. It will include a detailed treatment of the basic laws and theories, and a brief descriptive treatment of the common elements and compounds, in the latter part of the course emphasis will be placed on the writing of chemical equations and on the study of chemical equations and on the study of equilibrium reactions in solution.

Daily, two lectures and one laboratory period.   Six semester hours.
                                                             Prof. CARROLL, S.J.

CHEMISTRY 2. GENERAL INORGANIC CHEMISTRY, I.

This course covers the first semester's work in introductory college Chemistry.

Daily, one lecture and one laboratory period.   Four semester hours.
                                                             Prof. GUERIN.

CHEMISTRY 3. GENERAL INORGANIC CHEMISTRY, II.

This course covers the second semester's work in introductory college Chemistry. Daily, one lecture and one laboratory period.   Four semester hours.

Prof. GUERIN.

CHEMISTRY 4. QUALITATIVE INORGANIC CHEMISTRY.

This course includes a detailed treatment of Ionization and Chemical Equilibrium, as appplied to the solution of electrolytes. Problem work is emphasized in lectures and outside assignments. Laboratory work will deal with the identification and separation of the common cations and anions, in the preparation for the analysis of inorganic unknowns, employing the methods of basic, acid and dry analysis.

Daily, one lecture and one and one-half laboratory periods.   Five semester hours.

Prof. FAGAN.

CHEMISTRY 5. QUANTITATIVE ANALYSIS.

Classroom work discusses the chemistry of metallic and non-metallic radicals in solution from the quantitative viewpoint with approved methods of identification and estimation. Comparative gravimetric and volumetric processes are studied. Problem work is emphasized both in formal recitations and in assignments to be done by the student outside of class, thus equipping him properly to evaluate analytical data obtained in the laboratory or found in the literature.

Daily, one lecture and one and one-half laboratory periods.   Five semester hours.

Prof. FAGAN.

CHEMISTRY 6. ORGANIC CHEMISTRY.

The general principles of Organic Chemistry and the preparation an properties of important classes of compounds both aliphatic and aromati are discussed in the lectures. The laboratory work includes the determination b various methods of the elements commonly found in organic compounds, the stud of reactions, organic synthesis, methods of manipulation, application of theor to laboratory technique and the preparation of important compounds by a seri of syntheses.

Daily, one lecture and one laboratory period.   Four semester hour

Prof. O'DONNELL.

CHEMISTRY 7. ORGANIC CHEMISTRY.

This course is a continuation of Chemistry 6 and deals mainly with t aromatic series of compounds and proteins.

Daily, one lecture and one laboratory period.   Four semester hou

Prof. O'DONNELL.

CHEMISTRY 101. BIOCHEMISTRY.

An introductory course designed to correlate the chemical knowledge of t premedical student in the field of chemistry with that presented in Medi

School. It is recommended for those who plan to attend Medical School, nurses and technicians.

Daily, one lecture and one laboratory period.   Four semester hours.

Prof. McGUINN, S.J.

CHEMISTRY 261. QUANTITATIVE ORGANIC ANALYSIS.

This is essentially a laboratory course in which carbon compounds are analyzed by the micro-technique. It will include determination of metals, carbon, hydrogen, nitrogen and halogens in organic compounds.

Daily, two laboratory periods.   Four semester hours.

Prof. McGUINN, S.J.

DRAMATIC ARTS

DRAMATIC ARTS 1. INTERPRETATIONAL DIRECTING.

Practical exercise and theory of the technique of acting and methods of instructing actors for the tributary theatre, with emphasis on significant posture, vocal usage, use of stage areas for effects, character subordination and emergence; rehearsal methods and different types of direction and interpretation; stylization in various art forms. Opportunities will be given each student to direct a play or plays; those concentrating on acting as such will be required to appear in the class plays, from which they may be chosen for public appearance in the exhibition play. The voices of the students will also be recorded and analysed.

Daily, 9:00-11:00, with additional   Prof. BONN, S.J.
          time at the option of the professor.

DRAMATIC ARTS 2. MODERN PLAY PRODUCTION.

A course in the elements of stagecraft from the standpoint of the director, conducted by means of lectures, discussion groups, individual conferences, laboratory demonstrations, and workshop practice. Problems will be worked out for all types of stages, and the student may present his own particular problem for discussion. Special emphasis will be placed upon modern theatre technique including lighting, with the professional as well as amateur approach receiving consideration. Supplementary lectures will be given on make-up, the elements of scene construction, and costume making. The voices of the students will also be recorded and analysed. At the end of the term a play will be staged in cooperation with Dramatic Arts 1.

Daily, 9:00-11:00, with additional   Mr. DUVEY.
          time at the option of the professor.

Note: Please consult, also, Choral Speaking, under the Department of Education.

ECONOMICS

ECONOMICS 5. PRESENT DAY PROBLEMS.

A fundamental course dealing with general factors of production, forms of business units, laws of price, taxation and labor, money and banking, and the function of the government in regulating and coordinating economic activity. The principles will be presented and illustrated in the light of changing American conditions.

Daily, 10:50-11:40.   Two semester hours.

Mr. BUCK.

ECONOMICS 6. PRINCIPLES OF ECONOMICS IN WAR TIME.

This course will cover a discussion of the traditional concepts of value and distribution, monetary policies, labor problems, and international trade and finance as affected by monopolistic regulation in time of war. A particular comparison will be made of the effects produced upon the economies of England, Germany, and the United States.

Daily, 11:45-12:35.   Two semester hours.

Mr. BUCK.

EDUCATION

EDUCATION 2. CHARACTER EDUCATION.

This course aims at three distinct objectives: first, a scientific study of character involving the definition of character, the aim of character education, and the bases on which any true system of character education must be founded; second, the establishment of principles determining the best possible method of character training; third, the investigation and the critical evaluation of modern theories and practices in character education.

Daily, 9:00-9:50.   Two semester hours.

Prof. Fox, S.J.

EDUCATION 5. PRINCIPLES OF EDUCATION.

A presentation and elucidation of the basic concepts and principles which serve as norms in guiding educational activity. The aim of the course is to study and confirm the validity of the proximate principles which should serve as the immediate determinants of teaching procedure. The validity of these proximate principles will be established by reference to the ultimate and philosophical principles of education.

Daily, 10:50-11:40.   Two semester hours.

Prof. Fox, S.J.

EDUCATION 9. LANGUAGE AND READING IN THE GRADES.

This course aims to provide the teacher with effective methods of teaching reading, oral and written composition by a consideration of the needs of the child at different grade levels. Actual results of the work of children will be employed to illustrate various degrees of skill and ability.

Daily, 9:55-10:45.   Two semester hours.

Miss HAVERTY.

EDUCATION 11. CHORAL SPEAKING, I.

Evolution of Choral Speaking. Its educational value and effectiveness in awakening in students poetic appreciation and a taste for literature. Choral Speaking as an aid in overcoming self-consciousness and developing a well modulated voice, clear enunciation and correct pronunciation; with special emphasis on the technique of Choral Speaking as a method of speech-training for use by the classroom teacher.

Daily, 10:50-11:40. Two semester hours.

Miss Gow.

EDUCATION 100. CHORAL SPEAKING, II.

Advanced Choral Speaking. Training the verse speaking choir. Discussions and planning of choral speaking programs according to age groups for classroom and auditorium activities. Choral Speaking as an approach to drama.

Daily, 11:45-12:35. Two semester hours.

Miss Gow.

EDUCATION 101. PHILOSOPHY OF EDUCATION.

The course includes a discussion of the agencies of education, the social environment of the child, the major problems connected with curriculum, organization, administration and methods of teaching. The true aim of education is outlined and some of the more conspicuous among the false or inadequate aims of education are examined and criticized.

Daily, 10:50-11:40. Two semester hours.

Prof. DOHERTY, S.J.

EDUCATION 129. HISTORY OF EDUCATION IN THE UNITED STATES.

The schools of Colonial America. Modifying influences and the evolution of public organization and state control. The development of administrative forms, institutional types and practices and the progressive expansion and adjustment of American schools to new conditions.

Daily, 9:55-10:45. Two semester hours.

Prof. KOEN, S.J.

EDUCATION 159. PSYCHOMETRICS.

An introduction to individual mental testing. Practical experience in giving tests. Survey of psychological methods of measuring human traits.

Daily, 10:50-11:40 Two semester hours.

Prof. KELLAR.

EDUCATION 184. THE TEACHING OF ENGLISH LITERATURE.

Methods in the teaching of English literature with special discussion of the teaching of the drama and of the essay in the secondary school will be presented. Special attention will be given to the interpretation of the printed page, and to means of stimulating pupils to a comprehensive reading program. The necessity of remedial work in the fields discussed will receive consideration, as also the general aids now in use in the classroom as auxiliaries to the improvement of the teaching processes in literature.

Daily, 10:50-11:40.   Two semester hours.
                                                              Dr. BUTLER.

EDUCATION 243.   EXPERIMENTAL EDUCATIONAL PSYCHOLOGY, II.

Nature and organization of traits, development, learning and retention.

Daily, 12:40-1:30.   Two semester hours.
                                                              Prof. KELLAR.

EDUCATION 245.   PSYCHOLOGY OF ELEMENTARY SCHOOL SUBJECTS.

The learning process and factors affecting achievement in arithmetic, writing, and the social studies.

Daily, 9:00-9:50.   Two semester hours.
                                                              Prof. KELLAR.

EDUCATION 299.   METHODOLOGY OF EDUCATIONAL RESEARCH.

A survey of the more important principles which underlie successful research procedure in education. The course treats the major approaches to problem-solving in education; the various instruments used for the collection of data; the forms observed in thesis-writing. This course is prescribed for all students majoring i Education.

Daily, 11:45-12:35.   Two semester hours
                                                         EDUCATION FACULTY.

ENGLISH

ENGLISH 3.   THE ART OF POETRY.

This course discusses Poetry as one of the Fine Arts, treating of its definitio characteristic qualities and its four elements: emotion, imagination, thought an expression. The various types of poetry, together with the different schools o poetic thought, are studied.

Daily, 9.00-10.45.   Four semester hour
                                                         Prof. P. COLLINS, S.J.

ENGLISH 4.   THE ART OF RHETORIC.

A discussion of the principles underlying the art of Oratory and the precep by which the orator should be guided. Application of these principles to select masterpieces of English Oratory.

Daily, 9:00-10:45.   Four semester hou
                                                              Prof. BEAN, S.J.

ENGLISH 7. ENGLISH PROSE COMPOSITION.

This course aims. at a study and practice in elegance of expression. The details
that make for literary greatness will be considered so that there may result a
growth in the stylistic value of one's own compositions, letters, etc.

Daily, 11:45-12:35.   Two semester hours.
                                                            Prof. FEENEY, S.J.

ENGLISH 131. ENGLISH LITERATURE OF THE EIGHTEENTH CENTURY.

A survey will be presented of the important poets and prose writers of the
eighteenth century including Defoe, Addison, Swift, Johnson, Pope, Thomson,
Gray and Burns. Consideration will be given to periodicals. Emphasis will be
placed upon the critical and social thought reflected in literature.

Daily, 9:55-11:40.   Four semester hours.
                                                            Prof. GROB.

ENGLISH 152. AMERICAN LITERATURE.

In this course the following American writers will be discussed in their work
and definite literary influence: Walt Whitman, Emily Dickinson, Louis Guiney as
poets; Mark Twain, Stephen Crane, Frank Norris and Jack London as novelists.

Daily, 11:45-12:35.   Two semester hours.
                                                            Prof. BRENNAN, S.J.

ENGLISH 208. ENGLISH DRAMA TO 1642.

Pre-Shakespearian and Elizabethan drama, except that of Shakespeare, is the
matter investigated. Special attention is given to the literature on the subject.

Daily, 9:00-9:50.   Two semester hours.
                                                            Prof. JOHNSON, S.J.

ENGLISH 221. THE ART OF SHAKESPEARE.

Shakespeare's plays as art, poetry, drama. Considerations of life, thought and
art based upon the plays, *Henry the Sixth*.

Daily, 9.00-9.50.   Two semester hours.
                                                            Prof. BERNHARDT, S.J.

ENGLISH 245. FRANCIS THOMPSON.

The chief poems of Francis Thompson will be considered. A comparative study
will be made of *Poems* and *New Poems* in content and technique. Special attention
will be given to unpublished manuscripts in the Boston College Collection of
Thompsoniana.

Daily, 10:50-11:40.   Two semester hours.
                                                            Prof. CONNOLLY, S.J.

GAELIC 231. GAELIC LITERATURE, 1000-1550.

This course will be given through the medium of English translation. No knowledge of Gaelic is required. The course will include: the religious writings of the
Irish bards, various translations into Irish from Continental literature, Irish lives

of Saints, bardic thought and content, and historical and social influences upon the literature of the time in such writers as reveal the highest development of the period.

Daily, 9:55-10:45.   Two semester hours.

Prof. J. E. MURPHY, S.J.

FRENCH

FRENCH 1.   ELEMENTARY FRENCH.

An intensive study of the French grammar, suitable readings and written themes, daily exercises.

Daily, 9.00-10.45.   Four semester hours.

Prof. L. FITZGERALD, S.J.

FRENCH 2.   INTERMEDIATE FRENCH.

A thorough review of French grammar, written and oral composition and the reading of French prose of moderate difficulty.

Daily, 11.45-12.35.   Two semester hours.

Prof. DESOLENNL

FRENCH 3B.   FRENCH DRAMA.

A reading, background and literary qualities of the eighteenth century drama. Readings will be taken from the *Maitre Guérin* of Augier and other selected plays.

Daily, 10:50-11:40.   Two semester hours.

Prof. HAYES.

FRENCH 131.   ORIGIN AND DEVELOPMENT OF ROMANTICISM.

A course in which Chateaubriand, Lamartine, and de Vigny will be studied and discussed. Conducted in French.

Daily, 9:00-10:45.   Four semester hours.

Prof. DEMANGELEERE, S.J.

GAELIC

GAELIC 1.   ELEMENTARY GAELIC.

Elements of grammar; greetings, proverbs, short stories. This course aims to give a basis for reading and conversation and to explain many words and phrases found in Irish songs and poems.

Daily, 11:45-12:35.   Two semester hours.

Prof. J. E. MURPHY, S.J.

GAELIC 231.   Gaelic Literature, 1000-1550.

This course will be given through the medium of English translation. No knowledge of Gaelic is required. The course will include: the religious writings of the Irish bards, the various translations into Irish from Continental literature, Irish lives of the Saints, bardic thought and content, and historical and social influences upon the literature of the time in such writers as reveal the highest development of the period.

Daily, 9:55-10:45.   Two semester hours.

Prof. J. E. MURPHY, S.J.

GERMAN

GERMAN 1. ELEMENTARY GERMAN.

This course is intended for students who have had one year or less of the language in the secondary schools. It will consist of extensive drills in the fundamentals of grammar and include the most important irregular verbs and idiomatic expressions. The subject matter to be covered corresponds to the first year of College German.

Daily, 9.00-10.45.   Four semester hours.

Prof. BOULANGER.

GERMAN 11. INTERMEDIATE GERMAN.

This course corresponds to the second year of College German. It will consist of a review of the German grammar, readings and translations from German into English, easy conversation and compositions.

Daily, 10.50-11.40.   Two semester hours.

Prof. LABOUVIE.

GERMAN 23. SCIENTIFIC GERMAN.

The purpose of this course is to familiarize the student with the reading of scientific German texts of special interest to their field of study.

Daily, 12:40-1:30.   Two semester hours.

Prof. BOULANGER.

GERMAN 191. GERMAN CONVERSATION AND COMPOSITION.

This course is intended for those who wish a practical knowledge of the language. Advanced compositions, collateral readings and reports are required. Special attention will be given to correct and idiomatic expression. Translations from English into German and German into English.

Daily, 11.45-12.35.   Two semester hours.

Prof. LABOUVIE.

GREEK

GREEK 1. ELEMENTARY GREEK.

An intensive study of the alphabet, phonetics, morphology and grammar for those who are beginning Greek. Suitable reading exercises will be given.

Daily, 9:00-10:45.   Four semester hours.

GREEK 3. Selections from the Olynthiacs.

This is a course in Greek oratorical composition. The principles of rhetorical composition are studied. Demosthenes is discussed both as a statesman and as an orator. This course presupposes preparation in elementary Greek and the reading of Greek.

Daily, 10:50-11:40.   Two semester hours.
                                                       Prof. Buckley, S.J.

HISTORY AND GOVERNMENT

HISTORY 2. Europe From Charlemagne to Boniface VIII.

A survey of European civilization from the ninth through the thirteenth century.

Daily, 12:40-1:30.   Two semester hours.
                                                       Prof. Harney, S.J.

HISTORY 22. Europe During the Era of Rationalism and Revolution.

A survey of European civilization from 1648 to the Council of Vienna.

Daily, 11:45-12:35.   Two semester hours
                                                       Prof. Geary, S.J.

HISTORY 143. Europe and Asia Between Two World Wars.

This course will trace national and international factors from Versailles to th Battle of Poland.

Daily, 9:55-11:40.   Four semester hour
                                                       Prof. Mahoney.

HISTORY 151. American History Survey, I.

A survey of American political and cultural history from the era of colonizatio through the Civil War.

Daily, 9:55-11:40.   Four semester hour
                                                       Prof. Doyle.

HISTORY 201. Science and Method of History.

In this course the fundamental nature of history is examined and establishe together with the principles of historical criticism that should actuate the stude and writer. This course is prescribed for graduate students in the Department History and must be taken by all who have not as yet fulfilled this requirement

Daily, 10:50-12:35.   Four semester hou
                                                       Prof. Burke, S.J.

HISTORY 299. READINGS AND RESEARCH.

A study of source material and authoritative secondary material for a deeper knowledge of some problems previously studied. The number of credits will depend on reports and examinations.

Prof. BURKE, S.J. and Prof. FINNEGAN, S.J.

GOVERNMENT 113. ROOTS AND POSTULATES OF AMERICAN DEMOCRACY.

This course will illustrate the interplay between freedom and authority in the American federal system. The current applications and fundamental philosophy of the Bill of Rights will be stressed.

Daily, 9:00-9:50.　　　　　　　　　　　　　　Two semester hours.
Prof. BURKE, S.J.

GOVERNMENT 242. THE NATURAL LAW IN THE HISTORY OF POLITICAL THEORY.

The evolution of the Natural Law theory of the state from Aristotle through St. Augustine, St. Thomas, Suarez, Edmund Burke to the present.

Daily, 11:45-1:30.　　　　　　　　　　　　　Four semester hours.
Prof. HIGGINS, S.J.

GOVERNMENT 299. READINGS AND RESEARCH.

A study of source material and authoritative secondary material for a deeper knowledge of some problems previously studied. The number of credits will depend on reports and examinations.

Prof. BURKE, S.J.

ITALIAN

ITALIAN 1. ELEMENTARY ITALIAN.

The work in elementary Italian comprises a careful drill in pronunciation, memorizing of idiomatic expressions, rudiments of the grammar, reading of Italian prose authors, translation of English prose into Italian.

Daily, 9:55-11:40.　　　　　　　　　　　　Four semester hours.
Prof. DE SOLENNI.

ITALIAN 2. INTERMEDIATE ITALIAN.

This course contains a thorough review of the grammar. Practice in composition, both oral and written, will be given special consideration. Plays and short stories by contemporaries will be read.

Daily, 9:00-9:45.　　　　　　　　　　　　　Two semester hours.
Prof. DE SOLENNI.

ITALIAN 181. ITALIAN COMPOSITION AND CONVERSATION.

The purpose of this course is to develop fluency and correctness in written and spoken Italian through translation and oral composition.

Daily, 12:40-1:30.　　　　　　　　　　　　Two semester hours.
Prof. DE SOLENNI.

LATIN

LATIN 1. LATIN PROSE COMPOSITION.

A course in Latin Prose Composition based upon imitation of the style of Cice
It will include study and practice in grammatical correctness, examination of
essential features of Latin expression, exercises in word order and a study of
structure of the Latin period.

Daily, 10:50-11:40.   Two semester ho
                                                         Prof. HERNE, S J

LATIN 3. THE ELEGIAC POETS.

The course will comprise selections from the works of Catullus, Tibullus,
Propertius, together with additional odes of Horace. Poetical forms, meters
literary influences will be studied.

Daily, 9:55-10:45.   Two semester ho
                                                         Prof. REINHALTER, S.J

LATIN 4. CICERO: PRO MILONE.

A study of the object, content, and historical background of Cicero's spe
in behalf of Milo and a discussion of the rhetorical principles exemplified in
argumentation of the speech.

Daily, 10:50-11:40.   Two semester ho
                                                         Prof. QUINN, S.

LATIN 101. LATIN SURVEY, I: TO THE CLOSE OF THE GOLDEN AGE.

The aim of this course is to give a comprehensive view of the field of L
literature, affording an opportunity for extensive reading and critical apprecia
of Latin authors from the earliest times to the close of the Golden Age.

Daily, 9:55-10:45.   Two semester h
                                                         Prof. R. SHEA, S.

LATIN 144. LATIN POETRY OF THE EMPIRE.

This course will comprise a study of the works of Persius, Juvenal, and Ma
Daily, 10:50-11:40.   Two semester h
                                                         Prof. McCAULEY, S.

LATIN 199. READING FOR PREREQUISITES.

Assignments in the reading of authors and related literature to be done u
direction by candidates who are deficient in prerequisite credits. The numbe
credits given will depend on the judgment of the director.

                                                         Prof. W. E. FITZGERALD, S.

LATIN 235. PLAUTUS.

A study of the language and style of early Roman Comedy, its developi
and influence on Latin literature.

Daily, 9:00-9:50.   Two semester h
                                                         Prof. MULCAHY, S

MATHEMATICS

MATHEMATICS 2. FRESHMAN MATHEMATICS, II.

Selected topics from Plane Analytic Geometry.

Daily, 12:40-1:30.   Two semester hours.
                                                    Mr. CEDRONE.

MATHEMATICS 5. SPHERICAL TRIGONOMETRY.

The theory and applications of spherical trigonometry.

Daily, 11:45-12:35.   Two semester hours.
                                                    Mr. CEDRONE.

MATHEMATICS 11. NAVIGATION.

The theory and practice of navigation.

Daily, 11:45-1:30.   Four semester hours.

MATHEMATICS 31. DIFFERENTIAL CALCULUS.

Fundamental notions of functions, limits, derivatives and differentials; differentiation of functions; applications, partial differentiation.

Daily, 10:50-11:40.   Two semester hours.
                                                    Prof. MARCOU.

MATHEMATICS 32. INTEGRAL CALCULUS.

Elementary processes of integration; integration by parts and other devices; applications; multiple integration.

Daily, 10:50-11:40.   Two semester hours.
                                                    Mr. CEDRONE.

MATHEMATICS 142. ADVANCED CALCULUS.

A more precise definition of function, derivative, continuity, etc. is given. The course will also treat: power series, partial differentials, implicit functions, curvilinear coordinates, the definite integral, line, surface, and space integrals.

Daily, 9:00-10:45.   Four semester hours.
                                                    Prof. MARCOU.

MATHEMATICS 165. POINT SET THEORY.

An introduction to the theory of plane sets of points.

Daily, 9:00-10:45.   Four semester hours.

PHILOSOPHY

PHILOSOPHY 1. DIALECTICS.

A fundamental course in Philosophy. As an introductory course its purpose is to train the student in the mechanics of thought and make him familiar with the principles of correct reasoning. To this end a study will be made of the major activities of the mind, namely, the Simple Apprehension, the Judgment and the process of Reasoning. The corresponding external expressions of these activities, namely, the Term, the Proposition and the Argument, will also be treated in detail. During the course examples of both correct and fallacious reasoning drawn from various sources will be offered for testing, and exercises will be assigned for practical application of the principles established.

Daily, 9:00-9:50, June 30-Aug. 8;   Three semester hours.
  9:55-10:45, June 30-July 17.   *Prof.* S. SHEA, S.J.

PHILOSOPHY 2. EPISTEMOLOGY.

A philosophical defense of human knowledge. The object of this course is to vindicate the cognoscitive faculties of man. This will involve a critical examination of various theories of knowledge concerning the nature, sources and criteria of truth. By the application of logical analysis the contradictions and inconsistencies of false theories will be exposed, and the soundness of the Scholastic position justified. During the course the following theories will be examined and criticised: Universal Scepticism, Cartesianism, Idealism, Kantianism, Traditionalism, Materialism, Rationalism and Christian Science.

Daily, 9:00-9:50, June 30-Aug. 8;   Three semester hours.
  9:55-10:45, June 30-July 17.   *Prof.* FRIARY, S.J.

PHILOSOPHY 3. ONTOLOGY.

Being, its objective concept. Essence. States of Being: Existence; Possibility, internal and external. Source of internal possibility. Kind of Being: Substance and Accident. Attributes of Being: one, true, good. Cause of Being. Perfection of Being: finite and infinite, contingent and necessary. Order and beauty of Being.

Daily, 10:50-11:40.   Two semester hours.
                                                     Prof. O'CONNOR, S.J.

PHILOSOPHY 4. COSMOLOGY. THE MATERIAL UNIVERSE.

An examination of the opinions advanced in explanation of the origin of the material universe: Pantheism, Materialism and Creationism. The theories of the intrinsic constitution of matter: Mechanism, Dynamism and Hylomorphism. The laws which govern the activities of physical bodies. The possibility and cognoscibility of miracles.

Daily, 11:45-12:35.   Two semester hours.
                                                     Prof. FLAHERTY, S.J.

PHILOSOPHY 5. FUNDAMENTAL PSYCHOLOGY.

A philosophical study of life in general. The purpose of this treatise is to establish ultimate truths concerning the nature and origin of life. This involves a study of vital phenomena variously manifested in the activities of plants, animals and man. The existence in every living being of a substantial principle of life essentially different from matter will be defended against the Mechanistic theory that vital action is simply the result of chemical activity. The true relations of this vital principle to the living body will be explained and defined. The question of rational life in brute animals will be discussed. Several lectures will be devoted to the origin of life and the origin of the species. The doctrines of Lamarck and Darwin and other evolutionary theories will be examined and criticised. This course will serve as a foundation for the following treatise.

Daily, 9:00-9:55.   Two semester hours.
                                                     Prof. BOEHM, S.J.

PHILOSOPHY 6.   ADVANCED PSYCHOLOGY.

A philosophical study of the human soul. The treatise will be devoted exclusively to a study of life in man, and will be restricted to those vital phenomena which pertain to the sensitive, intellectual and appetitive faculties The primary purpose of the course is to explain and defend the Scholastic doctrines concerning the nature, origin and destiny of the human soul; its secondary purpose is to explain and refute erroneous theories on these highly important questions. The lectures will treat the following: permanency of sense faculties, functions of the senses in the perceptive act, their relation to the mind in its perception of external material objects; existence of internal sense faculties; the nature of the soul, its substantiality and immateriality; the intellectual idea and its origin; existence of the will, and its freedom of choice; the soul as the substantial form of the body, its immortality and its production by the creative act of God. Various evolutionary theories offering to explain the origin of man will be carefully examined and criticised.

Daily, 10:50-11:40.   Two semester hours.
                                                       Prof. DUNCAN, S.J.

PHILOSOPHY 7.   NATURAL THEOLOGY.

God not Nature, nor Power behind Nature, nor World Soul or Spirit, but a Personal Being distinct from the Universe. Pantheism, Atheism, Agnosticism. The existence of God known not immediately, nor from intuition, nor by innate ideas, but by a posteriori demonstration. The essence and attributes of God: Self-existence, Necessity, Infinity, Eternity, Immutability, Immensity, Unity and Simplicity, Knowledge of God, Will of God. Action of God towards creatures: Creation, Conservation, Concurrence.

Daily, 11:45-12:35.   Two semester hours.
                                                       Prof. MOHAN, S.J.

PHILOSOPHY 8.   GENERAL ETHICS.

Definition, nature, object and necessity of Ethics; subjective and objective ultimate end of man; human action, its merit and imputability; morality of human acts; norm of morality, true and false; Utilitarianism and Hedonism; Mill and Spencer; external norm is law, eternal, natural and positive; nature and origin of moral obligation, human and divine; Kant's Categorical Imperative; internal norm is consciousness.

Daily, 9:00-10:45.   Four semester hours.
                                                       Prof. COTTER, S.J.

PHILOSOPHY 9.   APPLIED ETHICS.

This course treats of man's threefold relation, to his Creator, to his fellow man and to himself. The lectures will cover such topics as: worship, revelation, rationalism, indifferentism, self-preservation, suicide, direct and indirect killing, self-defense, lying, mental reservation and the professional secret. The right of private ownership will be defended. Strikes, trade unions, contracts, wills, the right and duties of Labor and Capital will be discussed. Other topics will include: Society in general, domestic society, parental authority, education of the child; civil society, its origin and purpose; functions of the civil government; state education; international law, nature and justice of war; pacificism; arbitration.

Daily, 9:50-11:40.   Four semester hours.

Prof. J. J. MURPHY, S.J.

PHILOSOPHY 10. HISTORY OF PHILOSOPHY, I.

This course will deal with the philosophy of Ancient Greece. After a brief study of the development of Greek Philosophy, the systems of Socrates, Plato and Aristotle will be studied in detail. The poetical system of Platonic Ideas, Aristotle's rational method, the comparison of the teaching's of Plato and Aristotle, and the acceptance of Aristotle's system as the basis of Scholastic Philosophy will be among the topics discussed.

Daily, 12:40-1:30.   Two semester hours.

Prof. McCARTHY, S.J.

PHILOSOPHY 113. KANT'S THEORY OF KNOWLEDGE.

A critical exposition of Kant's theory of Knowledge as presented in his *Critique of Pure Reason.* After an explanation of Kant's influence on modern thought, the *a priori* forms of space and time, the categories of the understanding, phenomena and noumena, synthetic *a priori* judgments, the transcendental unity of apperception, a detailed criticism of the theory will be presented.

Daily, 10:50-11:40.   Two semester hours.

Prof. HARDING, S.J.

PHILOSOPHY 131. SOCIAL PHILOSOPHY.

This course will treat the philosophy of property as found in the classical authors, such as Aristotle, St. Thomas and Locke. It will also discuss the concept of property as expressed in the labor encyclicals of Leo XIII and Pius XI and make application to modern socio-economic problems.

Daily, 9:55-10:45.   Two semester hours.

Prof. O'BRIEN, S.J.

PHILOSOPHY 201. ST. AUGUSTINE: DE CIVITATE DEI.

A reading and an analysis of the text of *The City of God,* both the Latin original and the English translations. Special attention will be given to the separation of the temporary from the timeless and to a discussion and application of St. Augustine's fundamental principles to our times.

Daily, 11:45-12:35.   Two semester hours

Prof. CAREY, S.J.

PHILOSOPHY 203. READINGS IN PLATO.

The text of Plato's dialogues will be used for class reading and discussion. The *Republic* will also be studied and its political implications analysed and criticis

Daily, 10:50-11:40.   Two semester hour

Prof. HABERSTROH, S.J.

PHYSICS

PHYSICS 1. MECHANICS AND HEAT.

A general college course of thirty lectures.

Daily, 10:50-11:40.   Two semester hours.

Prof. WHITE.

PHYSICS 2. LABORATORY COURSE IN MECHANICS AND HEAT.

This course consists of sixty hours of quantitative work on subjects given in Physics I. Reports, graphs and precision measurements are required.

Daily, 9:00-10:45.   Two semester hours.

Prof. WHITE *and Assistants.*

PHYSICS 3. ELECTRICITY, SOUND AND LIGHT.

A general college course of thirty lectures.

Daily, 9:00-9:45.   Two semester hours.

Prof. GAGER.

PHYSICS 4. LABORATORY COURSE IN ELECTRICITY, SOUND AND LIGHT,

This course consists of sixty hours of quantitative work on subjects given in Physics 3. Reports, graphs and precision measurements are required.

Daily, 9:55-11:40.   Two semester hours.

Prof. GAGER *and Assistants.*

PHYSICS 103. APPLIED MECHANICS,

The discussion of the mechanics of a particle and rigid bodies; the properties of elastic bodies; periodic motions.

Daily, 9:00-9:50.   Two semester huors.

Prof. WHITE.

PHYSICS 108. PHYSICAL OPTICS.

A study of wave motion and refraction, interference, polarization and the spectra of the elements.

Daily, 9:55-10:45.   Two semester hours.

Prof. REINHEIMER.

PHYSICS 111. ADVANCED ELECTRICITY.

This course first presents a brief mathematical review of direct current circuits in the transient and steady state as preparation for the main body of the course, a study of the alternating current circuits in the steady state utilizing the generalized network and circuit theorems.

Daily, 11:45-12:35.   Two semester hours.

Prof. GAGER.

PHYSICS 116. EXTERIOR BALLISTICS.

The methods of exterior ballistics including a review of certain concepts of mechanics, the construction and use of range tables, and the use of trajectories.

Daily, 11:45-12:35.   Two semester hours.

Prof. WHITE.

PHYSICS 121. RADIO ENGINEERING.

A treatment of radio transmitting and receiving systems including radio aids to navigation and avigation. The vacuum tube as an oscillator, amplifier, rectifier, modulator and demodulator will be stressed, and all applications will emphasize the communication aspect of national defense.

Daily, 10:45-11:40. Two semester hours.

Prof. GAGER.

PHYSICS 299. READING AND RESEARCH PROBLEMS.

Supervised problem and experimental work, and directed reading in Atomic Physics. Credit will depend on reports and examinations.

Prof. WHITE.

RELIGION

RELIGION 2. THE CHURCH OF CHRIST.

The arguments which prove that Christ founded a Church with certain definite characteristics. The nature and marks of that Church. The primacy and infallibility of the Pope. The bishops and their teaching office. The relation between church and state.

Daily, 10:50-11:40. Two semester hours.

Prof. McLAUGHLIN, S.J.

RELIGION 5. THE SACRAMENTS.

The subject matter of this course is the seven Sacraments. The nature of each Sacrament is discussed and the doctrine and practice of the Church in its regard is explained. Proofs of the divine origin of each sacrament are present from the traditional teaching and practice of the Church and from the inspire text of Holy Scripture.

Daily, 9:00-9:50. Two semester hours

Prof. DOUGLAS, S.J.

RELIGION 10. THE MODERN LIVES OF CHRIST.

The life and teaching of our Lord, Jesus Christ, as given in the recent works o Fillion, Lagrange, Lebreton, Prat.

Daily, 11:45-12:35. Two semester hours

Prof. J. COLLINS, S.J.

SOCIOLOGY

SOCIOLOGY 31. PRINCIPLES OF SOCIOLOGY, I.

An outline of Sociology as a science, serving as an introduction to advance sociological study. It offers a systematic view of social life and culture in thei structural and dynamic aspects. Parts I and II will be offered in alternate summer

Daily, 11:45-12:35. Two semester hour

Prof. FITZGIBBON.

SOCIOLOGY 111. SOCIAL CONTROL.

Social control considered as a social process by which the individual is mad "group responsive" and by which social organization is developed and maintaine The following subjects are stressed: institutions as control agencies; means social control; the weakening of social control as an element in social problem

. and control in our dynamic society.

Daily, 9:00-9:50.   Two semester hours.

Prof. FITZGIBBON.

SOCIOLOGY 113. RURAL SOCIOLOGY.

A survey of rural society, demonstrating the formative influence upon persons, groupings and culture patterns, which arises from environment, occupation, class structure, social interests, etc. Insistent agricultural problems are stressed, especially as they apply connections, culturally and functionally, between the rural and urban environments.

Daily, 9:55-10:45.   Two semester hours.

Prof. FITZGIBBON.

SOCIOLOGY 201. SOCIOLOGY OF THE FAMILY.

A study of the main types historically presented by the family, with a comparison of their respective strength and weakness. Function of the family as a primary unit of society followed by a survey of representative social values which tend to affect the family as to solidarity, vitality and permanence.

Daily, 10:50-11:40.   Two semester hours.

Prof. O'CONNELL, S.J.

SPANISH

SPANISH 1. ELEMENTARY SPANISH.

This course is intended for students who are beginning Spanish. It deals with the fundamentals of the Spanish grammar and the idiomatic expressions and the most important irregular verbs. This course corresponds to the first year of College Spanish.

Daily, 9:00-10:45.   Four semester hours.

Prof. AZUOLA.

SPANISH 2. INTERMEDIATE SPANISH.

This course corresponds to the second year of College Spanish. It deals with the review of the Spanish grammar and the readings and translations of the most important Spanish texts. It serves as an introduction to the masterpieces of Spanish Literature.

Daily, 10:50-11:40.   Two semester hours.

Prof. AZUOLA.

SPANISH 181. SPANISH COMPOSITION AND CONVERSATION.

This course will enable the student to acquire ease and fluency in expression and idiomatic Spanish through practice in composition. Collateral readings and reports are required.

Daily, 11:45-12:35.   Two semester hours.

Prof. AZUOLA.

SPANISH 301. SEMINAR.

The purpose of the Seminar is to permit students to engage in special studies. Some suggested topics are: Galdos, Mexican Literature, Readings in Contemporary Spanish American Literature, etc. Time and credit to be arranged.

Prof. AZUOLA.

SCHEDULE OF COURSES

Courses numbered 1 to 99 are for undergraduate students.

Courses numbered 100 to 199 are for advanced undergraduate and graduate stude

Courses numbered 200 up are for graduate students only.

9:00-9:50.

Accounting 21: Intermediate Accounting, I....................PROF. DRUMMEY
Dramatic Arts 1: Interpretation Directing....................PROF. BONN, S.J.
Dramatic Arts 2: Modern Play Production....................MR. DUVEY
Education 2: Character Education....................PROF. FOX, S.J.
Education 245: Psychology of Elem. School Subjects........PROF. KELLAR
English 3: Art of Poetry....................PROF. P. COLLINS, S.J.
English 4: Art of Rhetoric....................PROF. BEAN, S.J.
English 208: English Drama to 1642....................PROF. JOHNSON, S.J.
English 221: Art of Shakespeare....................PROF. BERNHARDT, S.J.
French 1: Elementary French....................PROF. L. FITZGERALD, S.J.
French 131: Origin and Development of Romanticism........PROF. DEMANGELEERE, S.
German 1: Elementary German....................PROF. BOULANGER
Government 113: American Democracy....................PROF. BURKE, S.J.
Greek 1: Elementary Greek....................
Italian 2: Intermediate....................PROF. DESOLENNI
Latin 235: Plautus....................PROF. MULCAHY, S.J.
Mathematics 142: Advanced Calculus....................PROF. MARCOU
Mathematics 165: Point Set Theory....................
Philosophy 1: Dialectics....................PROF. S. SHEA, S.J.
Philosophy 2: Epistemology....................PROF. FRIARY, S.J.
Philosophy 5: Fundamental Psychology....................PROF. BOEHM, S.J.
Philosophy 8: General Ethics....................PROF. COTTER, S.J.
Physics 2: Laboratory: Mechanics and Heat....................PROF. WHITE
Physics 3: Electricity, Sound, Light....................PROF. GAGER
Physics 103: Applied Mechanics....................PROF. WHITE
Religion 5: Sacraments....................PROF. DOUGLAS, S.J.
Sociology 111: Social Control....................PROF. FITZGIBBON
Spanish 1: Elementary....................PROF. AZUOLA

9:55-10:45.

Accounting 1: Elementary Accounting, I....................MR. BRYAN
Education 9: Language and Reading in the Grades........MISS HAVERTY
Education 129: History of Education in U. S.....................PROF. KOEN, S.J.
English 131: English Literature of 18th Century........PROF. GROE
Gaelic 231: Gaelic Literature, 1000-1550....................PROF. J. E. MURPHY, S.J.
History 143: Europe and Asia Between Two World Wars....PROF. MAHONEY
History 151: American History Survey, I....................PROF. DOYLE
Italian 1: Elementary....................PROF. DESOLENNI

Latin 3: Elegiac Poets————————————————PROF. REINHALTER, S.J.
Latin 101: Latin Survey, L————————————————PROF. R. SHEA, S.J.
Philosophy 9: Applied Ethics————————————— PROF. J. J. MURPHY, S.J.
Philosophy 131: Social Philosophy————————————PROF. O'BRIEN, S.J.
Physics 108: Physical Optics—————————————PROF. REINHEIMER
Sociology 113: Rural Sociology————————————— PROF. FITZGIBBON

):50-11:40.

Accounting 22: Intermediate Accounting, II—————— PROF. DRUMMEY
Biology 3: Genetics ————————————————PROF. DUBOIS, S.J.
Economics 5: Present Day Problems————————————MR. BUCK
Education 5: Principles of Education—————————PROF. FOX, S.J.
Education 11: Choral Speaking, I————————————MISS GOW
Education 101: Philosophy of Education————————PROF. DOHERTY, S.J.
Education 159: Psychometrics ————————————PROF. KELLAR
Education 184: Teaching of English Literature—————DR. BUTLER
English 245: Francis Thompson————————————PROF. CONNOLLY, S.J.
French 3B: French Drama————————————————PROF. HAYES
German 11: Intermediate German————————————PROF. LABOUVIE
Greek 3: Selections from the Olynthiacs————————PROF. BUCKLEY, S.J.
Latin 1: Prose Composition ————————————PROF. HERNE, S.J.
History 201: Science and Method————————————PROF. BURKE, S.J.
Latin 4: Cicero: Pro Milone————————————————PROF. QUINN, S.J.
Latin 144: Latin Poetry of the Empire————————PROF. McCAULEY, S.J.
Mathematics 31: Differential Calculus————————PROF. MARCOU
Mathematics 32: Integral Calculus————————————MR. CEDRONE
Philosophy 3: Ontology ————————————————PROF. O'CONNOR, S.J.
Philosophy 6: Advanced Psychology————————————PROF. DUNCAN, S.J.
Philosophy 113: Kant ————————————————PROF. HARDING, S.J.
Philosophy 203: Plato ————————————————PROF. HABERSTROH, S.J.
Physics 1: Mechanics and Heat————————————PROF. WHITE
Physics 121: Radio Engineering————————————PROF. GAGER
Religion 2: Church of Christ————————————PROF. McLAUGHLIN, S.J.
Sociology 201: Sociology of the Family————————PROF. O'CONNELL, S.J.
Spanish 2: Intermediate ————————————————PROF. AZUOLA

:45-12:35.

Accounting 2: Elementary Accounting, II—————— MR. BRYAN
Biology 4: Hygiene ————————————————MR. RYAN
Economics 6: Principles of Economics in War Time———— MR. BUCK
Education 100: Choral Speaking, II————————————MISS GOW
Education 299: Methodology of Educational Research——EDUCATION FACULTY
English 7: Prose Composition ————————————PROF. FEENEY, S.J.
English 152: American Literature ————————————PROF. BRENNAN, S.J.
French 2: Intermediate French————————————— PROF. deSOLENNI

Gaelic 1: Elementary Gaelic..Prof. J. E.Murphy, S

German 191: Conversation and Composition..................Prof. Labouvie

Government 242: Natural Law and Political Theory............Prof. Higgins, S.J.

History 22: Era of Rationalism and Revolution................Prof. Geary, S.J.

Mathematics 5: Spherical Trigonometry............................Mr. Cedrone

Mathematics 11: Navigation...

Philosophy 4: Cosmology ....Prof. Flaherty, S.J.

Philosophy 7: Natural Theology..Prof. Mohan, S.J.

Philosophy 201: St. Augustine..Prof. Carey, S.J.

Physics 111: Advanced Electricity....................................Prof. Gager

Physics 116: Exterior Ballistics..Prof. White

Religion 10: Modern Lives of Christ ....Prof. J. Collins, S.]

Sociology 31: Principles ....Prof. Fitzgibbon

Spanish 181: Composition and Conversation....................Prof. Azuola

12:40-1:30.

Biology 5: Physiology ....Mr. Maynard

Education 243: Experimental Educ. Psychology..............Prof. Kellar

German 23: Scientific German...Prof. Boulanger

History 2: Europe from Charlemagne to Boniface VIII......Prof. Harney, S.J.

Italian 181: Composition and Conversation....................Prof. deSolenni

Mathematics 2: Freshman Mathematics, II......................Mr. Cedrone

Philosophy 10: History of Philosophy, I..........................Prof. McCarthy, S.

Spanish 301: Seminar ....Prof. Azuola